HOW OUR LAWS ARE MADE.

TEACHING KIDS ABOUT CIVIC LITERACY

DEJI OLAORE, SANYA ONAYOADE & TUNDE OLAKUNLE

Printed in the United States of America

Book Design by Matilda Danso
First Printing: Jan 2021

ISBN–

Deji Olaore
E-mail: dejiolaore@gmail.com

CONTENTS

PREFACE

The sustainability of democratic government in any nation depends on its citizens' participation. It is the responsibility of every citizen to be involved in the country's political process. As part of the citizens' participation, people need to understand different structures/layers of government that exist, and how each layer functions. One of the fundamental functions of government is to protect lives and property; and to maintain laws and order.

Laws are made based on our values, norms, and universally acceptable principles. These laws are made at different levels of government such as the Local government, the State government, and the Federal government levels. It is important for every citizen to understand where the laws of the land come from, who the lawmakers are, how the laws are made and how you can contribute to the process of law making as a citizen.

This book provides readers with basic information about the origin of the Constitution, (which is the highest law of the land), the three branches of government – The Executive, the Legislature, and the Judiciary. It provides an overview of the three tiers/levels of government: the local government, the state government, and the federal government. Finally, the book explains the process of law making in Nigeria (particularly at the Federal level) and how citizens can contribute to the process. Citizen participation is an important element of good governance; therefore, every citizen has the right to participate in the political and governance process of the country.

THE CONSTITUTION

The beginning of a country starts with the Constitution. The Constitution spells out the rules and laws that govern a country, the type of government the country will have; the kind of people to occupy various positions in the government and their qualifications; the duty of elected people to the citizens of a country, and the duty of citizens to the country (are spelt out accordingly in the constitution). Some sources of the constitution peculiar to Nigeria are Acts of Parliament, Military decrees, the Executive Orders and Sharia law which is obtainable in most part of the northern Nigeria. We also have judicial precedents and landmark judgements as other sources of the constitution.

The Nigerian Constitution spells out the different levels of government and the arms or branches of government. There are three levels of government. They are: The Federal Government, the State Government and the Local Government. The three branches of government are: The Executive, the Legislature and the Judiciary.

In general, the Constitution explains how the President, the

Governor, the Local Government Chairman, and other elected officers should govern. It explains how legislators (or law makers) should make laws and how Justices, Judges and Magistrates in the judiciary should interpret laws.

The Constitution is the most powerful law of the land. The Constitution is 'Supreme' and its provisions are binding on all authorities and persons throughout the country. No other law of the land MUST go against the Constitution. Any law or its provision(s) that contradicts the Constitution is invalid and cannot be enforced because it is unconstitutional.

The Constitution provides for the distribution of powers among the three branches of government. This control of powers is exercised through Exclusive Legislative List, Concurrent Legislative List and Residual Legislative List.

The Exclusive Legislative List is assigned to the Federal Government alone with 68 items such as Accounts of the Government of the Federation, Aviation, Currency coinage and legal tender, Customs and excise duties, Creation of states, Census, Citizenship, Defense, External Affairs, Extradition. Military (including Army, Navy and Air Force), Passports and visas, Police, Posts, Prisons, Railway[1] e.t.c. (see Second Schedule Part I of the 1999 Constitution for full list).

Concurrent Legislative List contains areas where powers are shared jointly by both the Federal Government and state governments. For example: Allocation and revenue, Antiquities and monuments, Achieves, Collection of taxes, Electoral laws, Commercila or agricultural development, Universities, Technological and post primary education etc. (see Second Schedule Part II of the 1999 Constitution for full list).Though the constitution allows both tiers of government to make laws together, the Federal Government is supreme.

Residual list is reserved for powers not included in either the exclusive or the concurrent list, and has such items as traditional and chieftaincy matters, markets etc.

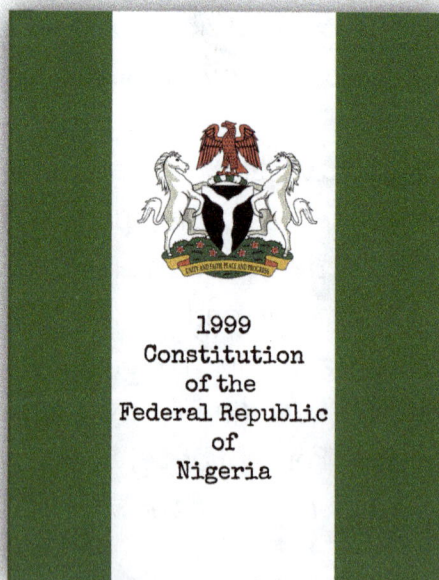

1999
Constitution
of the
Federal Republic
of
Nigeria

PARLIAMENTARY SYSTEM OF GOVERNMENT

At independence in 1960, Nigeria practiced Parliamentary system of government. This is because Nigeria got her independence from Britain which practices Parliamentary system.

Parliamentary system is a democratic form of government in which the party (or a coalition of parties) with the greatest representation in the parliament (legislature) forms the government. All decisions of governance are managed by a legislative body. The political party that wins the majority of seats in the legislative house forms the government and the leader of the party becomes the Prime Minister.

Executive functions are exercised by members of the parliament appointed by the Prime Minister to the cabinet. The parties in the minority serve in opposition to the majority and have the duty to challenge it regularly. Prime Ministers may be removed from power whenever they lose the confidence of a majority of the ruling party or of the Parliament[2]. This was the process that produced the first and only Prime Minister of Nigeria, Sir Abubakar Tafawa Balewa on October 1, 1960.

PRESIDENTIAL SYSTEM OF GOVERNMENT

Presidential System of government is a form of government whereby you have the President as the Head of Government, the Chief Executive of the Federation, and Commander-in-Chief of the Armed Forces; the Legislature (law making body) and the Judiciary (that interprets the laws). Nigeria first started practicing the Presidential System of government in 1979. Alhaji Aliyu Shehu Shagari was the first democratically elected President of Nigeria. He was the President of Nigeria from October 1, 1979 to December 31, 1983.

LEVELS OF GOVERNMENT

There are three levels or tiers of government. They are: the Federal Government, the State Government and the Local Government. Each one of them has three arms of government which are the Executive, the Legislature and the Judiciary.

The Federal Government

Nigeria's government is called the federal or national government. It provides services to all the people of Nigeria. It carries out different projects/programs for the benefits of the people. The Federal Government also ensures the provision of security of lives and properties of the citizens. There are 36 States in Nigeria and the Federal Capital Territory (FCT) Abuja. One State cannot make laws for another, so citizens from each State elect people to represent them at the National Assembly or the State House of Assembly. To represent means to speak or act on behalf of a person or a group of people. And this system of government is called DEMOCRACY. Democracy is defined as a government "of the people, by the people and for the People". A democracy means power is shared ʔy all the citizens.

The State Government

The State Government is an administrative level that is closer to the people than the Federal Government. A State Government provides services to all the people living in that State. Many Local Government Areas make up a State.

The State provides social services (amenities) that make life comfortable for the people. Such services include hospitals, schools, good roads, water and light. The Constitution also gives power to the State Government to supervise activities of the Local Governments within the State.

The Local Government

Each State has cities, towns and villages that are either broken down or grouped together to form the lowest administrative level of government called the Local Government Authority (LGA).

Every community belongs to a Local Government. The Local Government is the closest government to the people, that is why it is referred to as 'grassroots' government. A Local Government provides services that benefit the people living in the Local Government Area. The Constitution also gives power to Local Governments to supervise primary schools, motor parks, markets, marriage registry, healthcare and community development associations. There are 774 local governments in Nigeria.

Elected Councilors at the Local Government make laws (called Bye-Laws) for the people living within the Local Government Area.

BRAIN WORK #1

Who is the current President of Nigeria?

[   ]

What political party does he belongs to?

[   ]

Who was the first democratically elected President of Nigeria?

[   ]

When was he elected as the President of Nigeria?

[   ]

Who is the Chief Justice of Nigeria (CJN)?

[   ]

What is the name of the Senate President?

[   ]

Who is the Speaker of House of Representatives?

[   ]

Where is the capital of Nigeria?

[   ]

CITIZENSHIP

Who is a citizen?

A citizen is a person who is born in a country or who has earned the right to become a member of the country by law. A good citizen is therefore the one who obeys the law of his/her country. He does good things and encourages others to do same.

Rights and Responsibilities of a Citizen

As a citizen of Nigeria, you have certain rights and responsibilities. These rights and responsibilities are defined in Chapter 4 Sections 33-44 of the 1999 Constitution (as amended) of the Federal Republic of Nigeria. Some of the "Fundamental Rights" are:

- Right to life.
- Right to dignity of human persons.
- Right to personal liberty.
- Right to fair hearing.
- Right to privacy.
- Right to freedom of thought, conscience, and religion.
- Right to freedom of expression.
- Right to freedom of movement.
- Right to freedom from discrimination.
- Right to property ownership.

Similarly, Chapter 2 Section 24 of the 1999 Constitution of the Federal Republic of Nigeria spelt out the responsibilities of a citizen as follows:

- Obey the law/constitution
- Pay Taxes
- Respect for National Flag; National Pledge and Legitimate Authority.
- Enhance the power, prestige, and good name of Nigeria.
- Respect the dignity of other citizens and their rights.
- Promote the spirit of common brotherhood and good neighborliness.
- Perform civic responsibilities such as voting and rendering national service.

Good Citizen and Political Participation

Every citizen has the right to participate in government. This is done by voting if the person has reached the age of 18 years. This is the age the Constitution allows a citizen to vote in Nigeria. Any citizen, whether below or over 18 years can also participate in government by writing letters to his/her Councilor, Local Government Chairman, Governor or any elected official such as a Representative or a Senator. He or she can also attend public gatherings where government policies and programs are discussed to make contributions on things that are going on in the communities. Such gatherings include Town Hall Meeting or a "Public Hearing" which National Assembly and State Houses of Assembly organize on every Bill to request for contributions from the citizens. If you have an idea that could improve your community, write to your Local Government Chairman or the State or Federal Legislator representing your area.

Community leaders listen to what the citizens say. They work with the citizens to try to make their community a better place to live.

Every member of a community can make a difference, including children. Good citizens obey the laws of the land and take interest in the activities of their government. You can write your Chairman/Governor today and tell him/her about your idea that can improve the condition of the people and the children in your community.

Be a good citizen. Clean your environment and pay your tax

The Right To Vote

Voting is a process by which citizens elect their leaders. It can be by thumb printing or marking on a paper or the symbol or photograph of the person of your choice. To elect means to choose by voting. Before a person can be allowed to vote, he or she must be a Nigerian citizen, and be at least 18 years old.

Voting is a special right. There are people in many parts of the world who do not have the rights or freedom to vote. In Nigeria, everyone who is 18 years and above has the right to vote. Only the prisoners cannot vote in Nigeria.

Campaign Rally

Voting is fun, too! You go behind a curtain to vote secretly and choose your leader. When citizens vote, they are voting for a candidate or political party of their choice.

A candidate is a person who seeks or is nominated to contest for a particular position at the Local Government, State Government or Federal Government level.

Perform your civic responsibility:
Don't forget to vote

BRAIN WORK #2

VOTE	OBEY	ELECT
CHANGE	CITIZEN	RIGHTS
WRITE	VOICE	IDEA
LAWS	GOOD	WORK
		FREEDOM

A	Z	V	O	I	C	E	F
X	R	O	B	E	Y	K	R
C	I	T	I	Z	E	N	E
H	G	E	L	E	C	T	E
A	H	I	A	G	O	O	D
N	T	D	W	O	R	K	O
G	S	E	S	X	L	B	M
E	V	A	W	R	I	T	E

BRANCHES OF GOVERNMENT

There are Three branches of government. They are: the Executive, the Legislature and the Judiciary. Each level of government (Federal, State and Local Government) has 3 arms of government.

The Federal Government

THE EXECUTIVE: The Executive Branch of the Federal Government is represented by the President who is also the Commander-in-chief of all the Armed Forces that is: the Army, Navy, Airforce and the Police. The President enforces the laws made by the legislature (also called the National or State Assembly). The President also has power to enter into political, economic, cultural and social agreements (treaties) on behalf of the country with any other country or organization. He or she signs or vetoes (rejects) laws passed by the Legislature.

The President appoints Ministers and Special Advisers who assist him/her in running the affairs of the country.

Election as a President

The Constitution states the qualifications needed to serve as a President.

To become the President of Nigeria, a person must:

- be a citizen of Nigeria by birth.
- be at least 35 years old
- be a member of a political party and is sponsored by that party
- be educated up to at least Secondary School level or its equivalent

If elected, the President will hold office for a term (period) of four years, together with a Vice- President who is chosen for the same term.

After the expiration of his or her first term, the President can also re-contest for another period of four years. This means the President can only be re-elected twice for a total period of eight years.

The President is the Head of State, the Chief Executive of the Federation and Commander-in-Chief of the Armed Forces of the federation.

THE LEGISLATURE: The National Assembly represents the Legislative branch of the Government. It is made up of two Chambers, the Senate Chamber, and the House of Representatives Chamber. A Member of the Senate is called "Senator", and a Member of the House of Representatives is addressed as "Honorable Member." The Constitution empowers the National Assembly to make laws for the whole country. The National Assembly also monitors or supervises the activities of the Executive to ensure that public funds are well used for the benefits of the citizens.

The National Assembly

There are 469 men and women who serve as Members of the National Assembly (109 Senators and 360 Representatives). Members meet at the National Assembly Complex, Abuja. The House of Representatives meets in the House Chamber and the Senate meets in the Senate Chamber. When the Senate or the House of Representatives is in session (a meeting), you can watch them debate either from the gallery of the National Assembly or from your Television.

National Assembly Complex

The Constitution states the qualifications needed to serve as a member of the National Assembly.

To serve as a member of House of Representatives, you must:
- be a citizen of Nigeria
- be at least 25 years old
- be a member of a political party and is sponsored by that political party
- be educated up to at least School Certificate level or its equivalent

Representatives are elected by the people of their constituency (area).

The House of Representatives is made up of 360 members elected from the 36 states plus Abuja. The number of elected Representatives from a State depends on its population (how many people live in an area). To find out how many people live in each State, the government takes a count of the population every ten years. This head count is called census. Each Representative is elected for a term of four years. S/he can be re-elected for more than one term.

To serve as a Senator, you must:
- be a citizen of Nigeria
- be at least 30 years old
- be a member of a political party and is sponsored by that party
- be educated up to at least School Certificate level or its equivalent

Senators are elected by the people of their State.

The Senate is made up of 109 members; three Senators are elected from each State and one Senator is elected to represent the Federal Capital Territory, Abuja. Each Senator is elected for a term of four years. S/he can be re-elected for more than one term. Senators represent the interest of their States. Equal number of Senators are elected from the States in order to make each State feel equal to the other.

BRAIN WORK #3

How many Chambers are in the National Assembly?

5	☐
6	☐
3	☐
2	☐
4	☐

Give the names of the Chambers in the National Assembly

_____

_____

What is the age qualification before you can contest as a Senator in Nigeria?

_____

What is the age qualification before you can contest as Member of House of Representatives?

_____

How many Senators are elected from each state?

_____

The House Chamber

Welcome to the House Chamber. Here is where the 360 Members of the House of Representatives meet. The House Chamber is bigger than the Senate Chamber. This is because the number of people in the House of Representatives is more than those in the Senate.

Members of the House of Representatives are elected to represent the people and the interest of their areas (Constituency). They are more than the Senators because they are supposed to be closer to the people and consult or ask them their opinions on issues of interest or importance to them.

The House Chamber

At the front of the room (Chamber) sits the Speaker of the House. Immediately in front of the Speaker is the Clerk of the House who keeps record of debate on the floor of the House. There is also the Sergeant-at-Arm who carries the Mace in front of the Speaker as he/she enters or leaves the House Chamber. Sergeant-at-Arm also maintains law and order during and after the debate in the House Chamber. The Speaker is usually elected from the majority party by his colleagues. (Majority party is the political party with the highest number of seats/members). When the House is in session, visitors can sit in the gallery and watch the Representatives debate.

The Mace

The Mace is a symbol of authority. Without it, the House cannot sit. Even if it sits, all decisions taken without the Mace lying in front of the Speaker is "null and void." That means they are not acceptable.

The Senate Chamber

Welcome to the Senate Chamber. At the front of this room (Chamber) sits the Senate President. Immediately in front of the Senate President are the Senate Clerks who keep records of Senate debate. There is also the Sergeant-At-Arm who carries the Mace in the front of the Senate President as he/she enters or goes out of the Senate Chamber. Similarly, the Sergeant-at-Arm also maintains law and order during and after the debate in the Senate Chamber.

The Senate Chamber

The other members of the Senate sit at assigned desks. The Senate President is usually elected from the majority party in the Senate by his colleagues. When the Senate is in session, visitors may sit in the gallery and watch the Senators debate.

Write the names of the three Senators that represent your state.

1.

2.

3.

How many different words can you make from the word SENATOR?

I made eight. Can you put them in alphabetical order?

SNORE   ANTS   SEAT   EAT

ROTTEN   NEAT   TORE

How many Senators are in the Senate?

How many Members are in the House of Representatives?

THE JUDICIARY

The judicial branch is represented by the courts. The courts are the Federal High Courts, Federal Court of Appeal, and the Supreme Court. The courts interpret the laws and decide if laws passed by the National Assembly are in line with the Constitution which is the supreme law of the land. The Supreme Court is the highest court of the land.

The Supreme Court is currently made up of sixteenth Judges including the Chief Justice of Nigeria.

The appointment of a person to the office of Chief Justice of Nigeria is made by the President after a recommendation of the National Judicial Council. The appointment has to be confirmed by the Senate. Also, the appointment of a Judge to the Supreme Court is made by the President after the recommendation of the National Judicial Council. He or she must also be confirmed by the Senate. Supreme Court Judges are called Justices.

Judges

The State Government

THE EXECUTIVE:

The Executive Branch is represented by the Governor who enforces laws that the State legislators make in the state. The Governor performs several duties including implementation of economic and social programs that benefit the citizens of the state. He signs or vetoes (rejects) laws passed by the state legislature.

The Governor appoints people to assist him in the administration of the state. Such people include Secretary to the State Government, Commissioners and Special Advisers.

Election as a Governor

A person shall be qualified for election as a Governor

- If he is a citizen of Nigeria by birth
- If he has attained the age of 30 years
- If he is a member of a political party and is sponsored by that party
- If he has been educated up to at least school certificate or its equivalent

He can be elected for a term of four years and re-elected for another term.

THE STATE LEGISLATURE: Unlike the legislative branch of the Federal Government, the State legislative branch is made up of one Chamber called House of Assembly. It is headed by a Speaker who is normally elected by his colleagues in the majority party (that is political party with the highest number of seats/members). A Member of the House is addressed as Honorable Member. The House of Assembly makes laws for the government and people of the state. The House of Assembly also monitors or supervises the activities of the state executive so that the state's resources could be used for the benefits of the people of that state. The number of legislators a House of Assembly has is based on the number of local governments in the State.

Election as House of Assembly member:
An elected Member can serve for a term of four years and can serve more than one term. To be elected, a candidate must be:
- A citizen of Nigeria
- Has attained the age of 25 years
- Has been educated up to at least School certificate level or its equivalent
- He is a member of a political party and is sponsored by that party

THE JUDICIARY: The head of the State Judiciary is the State Chief Judge. He is appointed by the State Governor. He/she must be confirmed by the state House of Assembly. Other judges are also appointed through the same process. The courts at the state level are State High Courts and Magistrate Courts.

Local Government

THE EXECUTIVE: The Chairman is usually the head of a Local Government and is elected by the citizens who live in the community. The Chairman enforces laws that the legislators in the Local Government make for the area. He signs or vetoes (rejects) laws passed by the state legislature. To assist the Chairman in the administration of the Local Government are different Heads of Department.

THE LEGISLATURE: The legislative arm of the Local Government has Councilors who meet to make what is called bye-laws. The legislature has a Leader of the House (who functions like a Speaker), Deputy Leader, Majority Leader and Minority Leader. Members of the legislature are called Councilors. A Councilor is elected for a term of 3 years and can be re-elected again for a second term.

Local Government Councilors

THE JUDICIARY: The Judicial arm of the Local Government is not as prominent as the other levels of government, but a court that serves the Local Government level is called the Customary Court. Customary court handles mainly small offences and marital problems in a Local Government area. It is the lowest court of the land.

BRAIN WORK #5

Who is the Governor of your State?

When was he elected?

How many members are in your state House of Assembly?

Where is the capital of your state?

Give the names of the states that have the following cities as their capitals:

Ikeja is the capital of?

Asaba is the capital of?

Ibadan is the capital of?

Lokoja is the capital of?

Awka is the capital of?

Kano is the capital of?

Benin City is the capital of?

Osogbo is the capital of?

Sokoto is the capital of

Calabar is the capital of

What is the name of your Local Government Chairman?

WRITE TODAY: Your Chairman, legislator and governor are interested in hearing from you. Do you have an idea that could make your state or local government a better place to live?

AN IDEA FOR A LAW

We have learnt about the legislative arm of each level of government. Now let us consider how our laws are made. It is important to note that the laws made at the Local Government levels only affect the people living in that Local Government area and the laws made in any State will only have effect on people living or/and working in that State. However, the laws made by the National Assembly affect all Nigerian citizens. Our next focus shall be on the process of law making at the National Assembly.

The National Assembly is the highest law-making body in the country. The National Assembly has two Legislative Chambers – The Senate and the House of Representatives. That means Nigeria operates a bi-cameral system of legislature. The two Chambers are empowered by the Nigerian Constitution to make laws for the peace, security as well as good and orderly administration of the country.

A law starts with an idea called a "Bill". What is a Bill? A Bill is a draft proposed law to be discussed by Members of the National Assembly. Anyone can suggest an idea for a law, but only the National Assembly can turn that idea into a law. Many Bills that are introduced into the National Assembly are ideas sent to the Members of the Assembly by the government, professional bodies, (lawyers, journalists, engineers, etc), business people, parents, civil society organizations, and even children.

Okay, my friend, it is now time to learn how a Bill becomes a law.

HOW A BILL BECOMES A LAW
(National Assembly)

Several Bills are introduced at the National Assembly, but not all the Bills become laws. A Bill may be introduced in either House of the National Assembly -i.e. the Senate or the House of Representatives. When a Bill is passed by the House in which it originates, it shall be sent to the other House for concurrence (or agreement). When the Bill is passed by the two Houses, the Bill will then be sent to the President for assent. Before a Bill becomes a law, it must be read three times (it has to go through different stages of legislative processes).

Now, follow these 8 steps to learn how a Bill becomes a law:

1. **First Reading:** A Bill is introduced

A Bill is introduced into the Senate or House of Representatives by a Member of the National Assembly. At the introductory/first reading stage, only the TITLE of the bill is read without any debate on it. Bills are either numbered as "H.B." to indicate a House Bill or "S.B" for a Senate Bill.

2. **Second Reading:**

At the second reading stage, the sponsor of the bill presents the general principles of the bill, canvasing the need to be supported to pass beyond this stage to becoming an Act of the National Assembly. Here other legislators speak for and against the bill. If it gains the support of majority, then it is referred to the appropriate Committee[s]which has/have legislative jurisdictions over such matters.

3. **Committee Stage:**

Here, the real legislative scrutiny of the bill is professionally handled by members of the relevant Committee[s] with jurisdiction over the proposed bill. The Committee will call for submissions/memoranda from stakeholders which might include professional bodies, pressure groups/NGOS and other interested parties whose passage of the bill would have future effect on their personal, collective, and or business life.

At this stage, the Committee may consider calling for a Public Hearing from relevant stakeholders to lend professional expertise and guide towards a successful scaling through of the bill. However, it is not all bills before the Committee that would require public hearings.

4. **Reporting Stage:**

The committee after collating the submissions of stakeholders from the public hearings will present the clean copy of the report to the whole House where it would be slated for the Third reading.

5. **Third Reading:**

At this stage, the Rules and Business Committee returns the Bill to the Chamber where it started (either in the House or Senate). When that Chamber's leader decides to call up (bring the Bill onto the floor), members dissolved into Committee of the whole (discuss the reasons for and against) the Bill, considering it clause by clause, change or amend it, and vote for either passing or rejecting it.

6. Bill Concurrence:

After a Bill is passed by one Chamber, it is sent to the other Chamber where it usually follows the same process as it did in the originating Chamber. In some instances, the receiving Chamber may pass the Bill as received; amend certain provisions of the Bill or reject the Bill completely.

7. Joint Conference Committee:

A Bill must be passed in identical form by both Houses. If a Bill is passed in both Houses (Senate and the House of Representatives) but there are differences between the version of the Bill passed in the Senate and the one Bill passed in the House of Representatives, a Joint Conference Committee is formed by the two Houses. The Conference Committee will be made up of Members from both Houses. The Conference Committee will work together to resolve the difference(s) and rewrite the Bill.

Members of the two Houses will vote to accept the report of the Conference Committee.

A "yes" vote passes the Bill while A "no" vote rejects the Bill. When both Houses passed the Bill in identical (the same) form, then it is sent to the President for approval and assent.

8. The President Decides

The President Approves the Bill.
If the President approves the Bill, he signs it into law, known as ASSENT'

The President Vetoes the Bill: If the President vetoes (rejects) the Bill, then the Bill is sent back to the Assembly with Mr. President's comments/reasons for rejecting the Bill. If both Houses (Senate and House of Representatives) passed the Bill by a two-third majority vote, the Bill becomes a law and the assent/signature of the President shall not be required.

If the President Does Not Sign or Veto the Bill:

If the President does not sign or vetoes the Bill within 30 days after the Bill was presented to him, the Bill becomes a law without the President's signature. However, if the National Assembly is not in session within those 30 days, the Bill fails to become a law.

Summary of How A Bill Becomes a Law

This is the summary of how a Bill Becomes a Law in Nigeria:

What is a Bill?

> A Bill is a draft proposed law to be discussed by Members of the Legislature (National Assembly or State House of Assembly.

Sources (origin) of Bills

1. A Bill can originate from the Executive or Judiciary (Executive Bills)
2. A Bill can come from Members of the Legislature (Private Member's Bill)
3. A Bill can also be an idea from Interest Groups/CSOs (through a Member of Parliament)

Stages for Passage of a Bill

i. First Reading
ii. Second Reading
iii. Committee Stage (Referral to a Standing Committee). The Committee can hold Public Hearing on a Bill to gather contributions and suggestions from the public and experts in this field if required.
iv. Reporting and Debate by Committee of the Whole House
v. Third Reading and passage of the Bill
vi. TBill Concurrence (The Bill must be passed by the two Chambers)
vii. Joint Conference Committee (if required)
viii. Assent by the President

BRAINWORK #6

It is time to test your brain power. These questions are difficult, so be sure and THINK before you answer them.

1. The head of state government is the:

　☐ Chairman　☐ Governor　☐ President

2. How many men and women serve as Members of the National Assembly?

　☐ 200　☐ 469　☐ 360

3. How many Senators may each state elect?

　☐ 10　☐ 3　☐ As many as it wants

4. A law starts with an idea called a:

　☐ Document　☐ Bill　☐ Constitution

5. If the President vetoes a bill, he is:

　☐ Rejecting it　☐ Approving the Bill

6. How many Senators are elected to represent the Federal Capital Territory (FCT), Abuja? ☐

7. Once A Bill is passed in the Senate, it automatically becomes a law. ☐ Yes ☐ No

RESOURCES

[1] 1999 Constitution of the Federal Republic of Nigeria.

[2] Encyclopaedia Britannica
https://www.britannica.com/topic/parliamentary-system
retrieved on July 24, 2020